Curiosities

of

Herefordshire

By the same Author:

Curiosities of Worcestershire (1991)

Curiosities

of

Herefordshire

A County Guide
to the Unusual

by

Ann Moore

S.B. Publications

To L.E.W. who gave me a love of history

First published in 1992 by S.B. Publications
Unit 2, The Old Station Yard, Pipe Gate, Nr. Market Drayton
Shropshire TF9 4HY

British Library Cataloguing in Publication Data
Moore, Ann
   Curiosities of Herefordshire:
   A county guide to the unusual.
   I. Hereford and Worcester (England) Curiosities
   I. Title
   914.24404

   ISBN 1-85770-007-4

Typeset and printed by Delmar Press (Colour Printers) Ltd., Nantwich, Cheshire

CONTENTS

CONTENTS

Page

CONTENTS

Front Cover: .... Grotto, Dinmore Manor
Half-title page: .... The Angel of Death, Abbey Dore
Page 1: .... Swan Mosaic, Ross-on-Wye
Back Cover: .... Misericord, All Saints Church, Hereford

ACKNOWLEDGEMENTS

Again I must offer thanks to those who have been so generous with their help: to Mr. Gartside of Ross and Mr. Delaney at Lucton Mill; to Mr. and Mrs. Pugh, Dr. Donald Hunt, Mrs. Richard Murray, Mr. Lindsey Heyes, Mr. Gareth Davies and Mrs. Patricia Hegarty; to Mr. and Mrs. Williams at Fownhope, to the incumbents of the churches and to the staff at Ledbury Tourist Centre. Finally my grateful thanks to Julie Meech and to Jonathan for his unfailing practical help and support.

Picture Credits: JM – Julie Meech. All other illustrations photographed by the author.

THE AUTHOR

Brought up in the Isle of Man, Ann Moore has lived in Worcester for the past twenty years with her two sons, now grown up. Since illness forced her to retire from teaching three years ago, she has had time to indulge in her hobbies of writing and a study of local history.

Her first book *Curiosities* of *Worcestershire* was published with great success in 1991. She is currently preparing other titles in this series of County Curiosities.

INTRODUCTION

As I have gathered the 'curiosities' for this volume, it has become more and more apparent how different are the two counties of Herefordshire and Worcestershire. The latter, on the whole has become more densely populated and busier. But here in rural Herefordshire, scattered along the border with Wales, one finds ruined castles, absent in Worcestershire. Here too, the many small rural communities have had no time for frivolities such as follies and elaborate houses, so that most Herefordshire 'curiosities' relate to daily life, to necessity, rather than to eccentricity or an urge to spend money.

Throughout the ages the Church has been the heart of the community. This is noticeably so in the rural areas of Herefordshire where they are often still the centre of life so that their precious furnishings remain to attract the curiosity seeker. I would ask that those seeking these 'curiosities' will recognise their value, so that they may remain for future generations to enjoy.

The list has been compiled using Hereford as a centre, and then moving clockwise from the north in the approximate directions of the compass; detailed map references are given in the text. I hope you will enjoy this personal collection – which is by no means definitive – and then go on to find more 'curiosities' of your own.

Ann Moore
Worcester

HEREFORDSHIRE

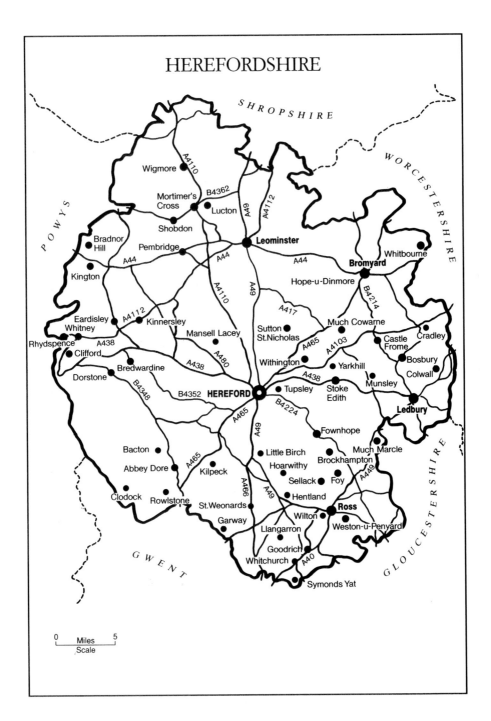

HEREFORD

HEREFORD CATHEDRAL

No-one could visit Hereford without admiring its magnificent Cathedral. Here is impressive architecture and stained glass, the world's largest chained library, ancient shrines and memorial brasses, great monuments and mosaics and the largest most detailed Medieval map in the world. Everyone knows of the Mappa Mundi, drawn on vellum by Hereford priest Richard De Bello about 1300 and showing Jerusalem as the centre of the world. In this book, however, I should like to point out other less famous, but equally interesting features which may be missed by the Cathedral visitor.

Photo: JM

One of the more unusual is a fireplace in the S. Transept. Early Medieval, it sits in the base of the west wall and one wonders how many – or how few – members of the congregation could have benefited from its warmth. There is only one other Cathedral fireplace in a similar position in England, and that is in Durham. For heating now, the Cathedral relies on several enormous gas-fired wrought iron stoves, the product of 'Gurney's, the London Warming and Ventilating Company', themselves of some historical interest.

The beautiful Triptych above the fireplace, depicting the Adoration of the Magi, is the work of the S.German (Swabian) school. It dates back to about 1530 and is unusual in showing so clearly one of the Magi as a black man.

HEREFORD

HEREFORD CATHEDRAL . . . 'IN DEATH NOT DIVIDED'.

Set in the floor of the south east Transept are the graves of a Dean and a Bishop, their life-long friendship denoted by these clasped hands. Herbert Croft (1603-91), a member of the ancient family at Croft Castle, was educated as a Catholic but later converted to the Church of England. He became chaplain to Charles I and then Dean of Hereford from 1644 to 1661 when he became Bishop. He was greatly respected for his charity and learning, and for more than 30 years worked with his friend George Benson who was Dean from 1672 until his death 20 years later. The friends died within a year of each other, and lie side by side here in their beloved Cathedral, 'in life united – in death not divided'.

Croft is also commemorated on the west front of the building in a medallion which records a momentous sermon he preached in 1645, condemning Cromwell's troops after they had taken Hereford during the Civil War.

Photo: JM.

3

HEREFORD

HEREFORD CATHEDRAL: PIGLETS

In the Lady Chapel these delightful little pigs trot happily round the arch above a memorial. It is the resting place of John De Swinfield, Precentor of the Cathedral from 1294 until his death in 1311. Resplendent in their cheerful blue and gold striped jackets, they are thought to be a pun on the Precentor's name, and it is refreshing to think that the family of so august a person showed a sense of humour which, centuries later, we may still enjoy.

HEREFORD

MISERICORDS

Location: All saints Church, Broad Street.
Map Reference: O.S. map 149 (1:50,000); 509400

The 13th-century Church of All Saints, perhaps best known for its crooked spire, stands like an oasis of peace beside the pavement in the middle of the city centre. Just two or three steps take one from the noise and bustle of this century into quiet, and the beauty bequeathed by the craftsmen of the past. This strange figure is one of ten 14th century Misericords set in two exquisitely carved oak canopied choir stalls. Here the carvings do not represent the seasons, as they often did, but include mice, birds and mermaids.

Other features of interest include a chained library of some 326 books in St Anthony's Chapel; a Jacobean pulpit (1621), magnificently carved to a Flemish design and costing when new, so we're told, £7; and a small 17th-century bread shelf. Here were kept small loaves, a bequest, to be distributed to 'Seven Poor Men after service every Lord's day'.

HEREFORD

UNIQUE FRIARS' CROSS

Location: In the rose garden behind Coningsby Hospital in Widemarsh St.
Map Reference: O.S. map 149 (1:50,000); 511404

For centuries people stood in all weathers beside this Cross, while raised above them and sheltered by its roof, a preacher led them in prayer and preached his sermon. It was built by 14th-century Friars in the cemetery of the Blackfriars Monastery, itself founded about 1276 and its church consecrated in the presence of Edward III and his son the Black Prince. The Cross survived when the Order was dissolved by Henry VIII, but was changed slightly during extensive restoration in 1864. Then Sir Gilbert Scott extended the stone rails to close off the entrance, originally a wooden gate through which the preacher entered. Nevertheless, it is an impressive piece of architectural history and is the only surviving 14th-century Friars' Preaching Cross in England.

HEREFORD

A RARE WAYSIDE CROSS

Location: On the western outskirts of the city at the junction of A438 and A4110.
Map Reference: O.S. map 149 (1:50,000); 493406

Standing proudly in the centre of a flower-decked round-about, the White Cross is a striking example of a 14th century Wayside Cross. Bearing the arms of Bishop Charlton, it stands on the site of an old temporary market at the City's boundary. Here during a time of plague 1361-2, provisions were left for the townspeople, for they could not be brought into the city. When the plague of the Black Death ended, Bishop Charlton erected the White Cross in thanksgiving. The Bishop (d.1369) lies beneath his tomb in the S.E. Transept of the Cathedral. Later 19th century restoration gave the cross a longer shaft than it originally had.

A folk tale tells of a ghost which once haunted the Cross. Old Taylor's ghost, worried because he had once moved a landmark, was often seen here riding a pony or sitting on a stile. It is said he was finally laid to rest by a man called Dennis, who, on the ghost's instruction, moved two large stones from one place to another. The ghost dis-appeared, but, so the story goes, Dennis was never the same again.

SUTTON ST NICHOLAS

WERGIN'S STONE

> *Location:*   1 mile north-north-east of the city, off A4103, 1¹/4 miles along the road
> to Sutton.
> *Map Reference:* O.S. map 149 (1:50,000); 530440

Almost certainly a pre-Christian monument, although no one is sure of its origin, Wergin's Stone stands aloof in a field to the right of the road on the way to Sutton. Unworked and about 4ft high, it is set into a base rather like a millstone with a tooled out cavity, perhaps once used for collecting rents or tributes. It is said that in the early 1650s 'the Devil' moved the stone '2 score paces' from its original place (which was possibly a meeting point for three boundary lines), and it took the strength of 9 oxen to pull it back. We shall probably never know its history, but the stone remains, fenced off, for us to look at and wonder about.

Photo: J.M.

HOPE-UNDER-DINMORE

THE HOME OF THE CATS EYE

> *Location:* 6 miles north of Hereford, 1 mile west of the main A49 to Leominster.
> *Map Reference:* O.S. map 149 (1:50,000); 476502

Dinmore Manor is the only house in England to have its name set out in 'cats eyes'. The sign is found at the end of the Manor's lane below the woods of Dinmore Hill – (the name coming from the Welsh 'dyn mawr' meaning the great hill). The sign is a neat reminder that the Manor was home to the late Richard Hollins Murray who, in the 1920s, invented these reflecting lenses which he patented in 1924. They were later developed by Percy Shaw of Halifax who put them in the self-cleaning rubber studs known to all thankful motorists as 'cats eyes'. In recognition of his invention Mr. Hollins Murray was made a life member of the Automobile Association.

HOPE-UNDER-DINMORE

THE GROTTO IN THE CLOISTERS

Location: 6 miles north of Hereford, 1 mile west of the main A49 to Leominster.
Map Reference: O.S. map 149 (1:50,000); 476502

Dinmore Manor and its gardens are well worth visiting, for there are many features of interest which cannot be mentioned here. The house is private but the gardens, cloisters and the 12th-century chapel are open all the year round. An excellent guide book is available which gives the history of this early centre of the military and monastic order of the Knights Hospitaller.

The lovely grotto at the junction of the Cloisters was created in 1926. The large Gothic-shaped window has been glazed with coloured glass which coincides exactly with the true horizon, and the grotto is an ingenious combination of coloured concrete set into chicken wire to form rocks through which the water bubbles. The whole effect is quite enchanting and very much more pleasing than any written description could suggest.

LEOMINSTER

THE PEOPLES' PRIORY

Here is the town situated between the rivers Lugg and Arrow, and once famous for its wool market, stands the beautiful Priory Church of St Peter and St Paul. The original Priory was founded in 660, and the beauty of the present building may now be enjoyed only because of the determination of the Leominster people.

In 1699 the church was nearly gutted by fire and plans were made to replace it with a smaller building. This so enraged the townspeople that they petitioned Earl Coningsby to listen to their views and offered £16,500 (a great deal of money in those days) toward the restoration of the Priory to its former glory. The building shows how successful they were, and the petition, although now faded, may still be read in the Priory. The work included restoration of the 3 Naves for which the church is famous – these built in the 12th, 13th and 14th centuries respectively, although the 14th century Nave was originally built as a south aisle.

Photo: J.M.

11

LEOMINSTER

THE STORY OF A NAME

Carved above the exterior of the Priory's West door are figures – illustration perhaps of the legend which, some believe, tells of the founding of Leominster. Merewald, a 7th century King of Mercia nicknamed 'The Lion', met a hermit, Ealfrid. They found that they had both had dreams which linked – Merewald dreamed of a Christian missionary bearing important news, and Ealfrid dreamed that a lion was eating out of his hand. The King was so impressed that he became a Christian there and then, and immediately founded a church and convent at the place where they had met – thus from AD 658, Leo-minster. Then again, the carving could just be a primitive picture of Samson and the Lion, and Leominster could be named after Earl Leofric, Lady Godiva's husband, who died in 1057, but who had re-endowed the religious community here. One has a choice.

Photo: J.M.

12

LEOMINSTER

A DUCKING STOOL

Kept safely in the Priory is this rare ducking stool, in perfect condition and one of only a few left in England in working order. 12 yards long when opened out and far from any pool or pond, it was last used in 1809 for ducking Jenny Pipes, a scold. If tradition was upheld then, she would have been strapped in the seat and paraded round the town before being 'ducked' (as was Sarah Leeke who was paraded in 1817, but not ducked). Stools such as this were also used as punishment for sellers of adulterated food.

LEOMINSTER

'WHERE JUSTICE RULE THERE VERTU FLOW...'

Not far from the Priory stands Grange Court, built at a time when Herefordshire was famous for its 6 Ws – Wool, Wheat, Wood, Water, Wine and Women. When it was originally built by John Abel the Master Builder, it took the form of a Butter Market. The lower part, now filled in, stood on 12 oak pillars and was the Market, while the upper storey was used as an Assembly Room. After standing for 2 centuries in Broad Street it was moved in 1853 to its present position and is now used as Council Offices. Above the arches is a long inscription, dated 1633, written in a jumble of Latin and English.

The line quoted above continues:

> *'Vive ut post vivas. Sat cito, si sat bene.*
> *Like cullumnes doo upprop the Frabrik of*
> *a building, So noble Gentri doo support*
> *the honor of a kingdom.*
> *In memoria aeterna erit Justus 1633.'*

LEOMINSTER

FOR WIDOWS ONLY

This quaint little man stands in a niche above a group of almshouses in the Bargate on the outskirts of the town. Rebuilt in 1874, the 'hospital' was originally erected in 1735 by a widow, Hestor Clark, and endowed at her death with £20 per annum. It was specifically intended for the use of '4 decayed widows', and one cannot help but wonder at the reasons for embellishing the building with this strange little man. he wears a cocked hat but little else, and holds a hatchet in his hand. The inscription makes one also wonder if Hestor had been badly used financially by her husband. It reads:-

'He who gives away all before he's dead,
Let 'em take this hatchet, and knock him on ye head'.

MORTIMER'S CROSS

HERE WAS A BATTLE. . .

Location: 7 miles north-west of Leominster at the junction of A4110 and B4362
Map Reference: O.S. map 149 (1:50,000); 425636

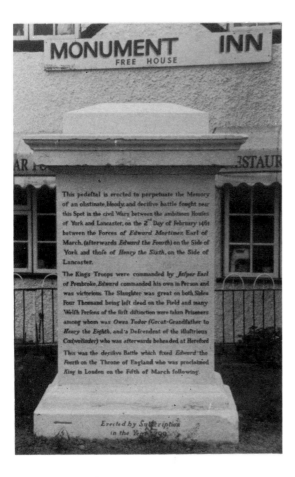

This monument to the Battle of Mortimer's Cross during the Wars of the Roses in February 1461, was set up in 1799. It stands close to the area used by the Lancastrian army for their camp. Here under the Earl of Pembroke and the red rose of Lancaster, they gathered to fight the 19 year old Edward Mortimer, Duke of York. It was a famous and bitter battle which ended when the triumphant young Duke marched on to London where, four months later, he was crowned King Edward IVth. Many of the 3800 casualties of the battle lie buried in a field, in a spot known as the 'clamp', to the south of the road leading from these `crossroads to Lucton; and it is difficult now to imagine the peaceful air rent, not by the noise of passing cars, but by the clash of steel and the screams of men and horses in battle.

LUCTON

A WORKING MILL

Location: 7½ miles north west of Leominster.
Map Reference: O.S. map 149 (1:50,000); 426637

A short distance to the north of the monument, Mortimer's Cross Mill splashes merrily in the sun. Built in the 18th century, it was in use grinding animal feed, until the 1940s and is still used occasionally to grind fodder for the rare breeds on Mill Farm. (These include the delightful Sebastapol (pantomime) geese, Dexter cattle, Golden Guernsey goats and various unusual breeds of sheep). The Mill's mechanism is on 3 floors and designed so that it may be worked by one man. Privately owned and in the care of English Heritage, the Mill is open between April and September on Thursdays, Sundays and Bank Holidays, between 2 and 5.30 p.m. There one may also see a new display showing the 4 stages of the Battle of Mortimer's Cross.

WITHINGTON

THIS IS THE ROAD TO HEREFORD. . .

> *Location:* 3¹/₂ miles from Hereford on the A4103 to Worcester at a turn off to Withington.
> *Map Reference:* O.S. map 149 (1:50,000); 565427

It is easy to pass this ancient milestone in summer, half hidden in grass beside a busy main road. Yellow and worn with age, it is the remains of the shaft of a wayside cross which in 1700 was turned upside down to form a milestone. It is now only with difficulty one can read the lettering on the west face of the stone –

THIS IS THE RO D TO HEREFORD TD 1700. (sic).

Formerly it told the distances to Worcester and Ledbury too. Standing just over 3ft. high, it has clearly never been 'white'. It is thought it was so called because it once stood on a Whiteway or common Salt Way.

MUCH COWARNE

I GIVE YOU MY HAND.

Location: 9 miles from Hereford off the A465 Hereford to Bromyard Road and 1¹/₂ miles from the main road.   *Map Reference:* O.S. map 149 (1:50,000); 619472

The church of St Mary the Virgin is tucked away down a country lane beside Paunceford Court and is said to be the geographical centre of Much Cowarne. But it also guards the effigy of a 13th century knight with an interesting story. Rather worn now, Grimbold de Paunceford lies clad in the Norman dress of a Crusader. In 1253 he married Constantia, daughter of John Lingen, a lady of means for she brought with her '6 score and 10 marks of money, 12 oxen, 100 sheep and 100 solidats' (rents of land) with a further 100 added by her father after the marriage ceremony. Later, however, Constantia gave far more than is normally expected of a wife.

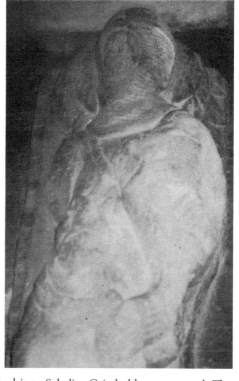

Grimbold in time followed his king to the Crusades where he was captured by Saladin. A message was sent to Paunceford Court that his release could only be secured if Saladin, in exchange for his prisoner, received 'a joint of his wyffe'. Whereupon Constantia sent for a surgeon from Gloucester Priory who cut off her hand above the wrist and dispatched it to Saladin. Grimbold was returned. The knight now lies alone in the south aisle of the church and his story could easily be dismissed as a romantic legend, but there is evidence of old 17th-century records which describe an altar monument to the de Pauncefords. The records say that they are both represented here, Grimbold as we see him now and Constantia with 'the hand and wrist cut off', these being 'carved close to the man's left side'. If only she had not disappeared altogether we could see for ourselves. One wonders where she went. The key to the church may be obtained from the house nearby.

WHITBOURNE

WHICH YEAR WAS IT?

Location: 5 miles from Bromyard off the A44 to Worcester.
Map Reference: O.S. map 149 (1:50,000); 725470

Photo: J.M.

This brass memorial is included because of its unusual dating. It is in memory of Elizabeth, the second wife of Richard Langford, Clerk, (and presumably a Curate at Whitbourne) who died aged 32 on 10th February 1708-9. It is difficult to explain why the year is uncertain unless the brass was erected some years after her death. At the time Elizabeth died, England unlike the rest of Western Europe, considered its new year to begin on Lady Day, March 25th. This meant that dates between 1st January and 24th March were considered as belonging to the previous year. It was not until 1752 that England conformed and began dating each year from 1st January. At that time people sometimes added OS or NS to denote that they referred to the Old Style or New Style dating. Perhaps it was then that the memorial was made, creating confusion as to the correct date.

Also of interest here at Whitbourne is a glass case containing a piece of a Cope, dating back to about 1500 and still retaining its crimson colour. It is thought that the Cope had been eventually cut up and adapted for used as an Altar frontal, but it must originally have been a magnificent garment.

20

YARKHILL

A SKEW BRIDGE.

Location: 8 miles from Hereford along the A4103 to Worcester, ¹/₂ mile along a lane to the right, signposted Monkhide.

Map Reference: O.S. map 149 (1:50,000); 612440

The patterns formed by the brickwork beneath the canal bridge at Monkhide are most unusual. When it was built in 1839 Stephen Ballard, the canal engineer, preferred to accept the challenge of building at an angle rather than change the route to accommodate a straight bridge. As a result, the bricks are placed diagonally from one corner to the other, forming a neat geometric pattern. It is a pity that the Hereford to Gloucester Canal network was never very successful, for few people have seen this example of Ballard's work, but it may still be appreciated by those who trouble to look.

CASTLE FROME

THE BENBOW POND

Location: 5 miles north-west of Ledbury at Hill Farm off B4214.
Map Reference: O.S. map 149 (1:50,000); 674454

A short distance away from Hill Farm, in a peaceful corner of a field where the only sound is of sheep grazing nearby, a small weed-strewn pool is a mecca for Mormans visiting from America. Here in 1840 Wilford Woodruff, an apostle of the Church of the Latter Day Saints, stayed with John and Jane Benbow at Hill Farm. In no time he had converted them to the faith, and many more followed. Between March and December he baptised more than 300 people, and with other evangelists had within 2 years converted 1200 others in the Malvern area. A plaque placed beside the pool, which is now owned by the church, commemorates the 150th anniversary of his visit. It quotes from his letter and shows Elder Woodruff 'clearing out a pool of water and preparing it for baptising'.

CASTLE FROME

THE MISERY OF EVIL.

Location: 6 miles north-west of Ledbury off the B4214.
Map Reference: O.S. map 149 (1:50,000); 668459

Hiding in a small country church which dates back to the Normans, is a piece of carving said to be 'one of the best pieces of Romanesque sculpture in England'. Over 800 years old and carved from a single block of sandstone, the font at St Michael's is the work of the Herefordshire school of carvers (see also Eardisly). The grotesque figures on which it rests, part animal and part human, are worn and broken now – perhaps fitting since they represent evil, while the carvings on the bowl above, symbolising the good of Christ, are still in good condition.

It is worth noticing too, on the mullion of a window in the chancel, a small near perfect bust of a Norman knight only a few inches high. He clasps his heart in his hand indicating a heart burial, probably in a recess below. When crusading knights were killed abroad their bodies lay where they fell, but the heart was sometimes sent home for burial.

23

CRADLEY

OBSERVE THIS LAW AND MARK IT WELL.

> *Location:* 3 miles west of Malvern off the A4103 Hereford to Worcester Road, 4 miles north of Colwall.
> *Map Reference:* O.S. map 150 (1:50,000); 735471

In the lovely Church of St James the Great at Cradley we see that bell ringers are left in no doubt as to the standards of behaviour expected of them. The bells, all 6 of them, hang 40ft above the ringers, suspended in a massive 17th-century oak frame. Originally cast by Abraham Rudhall of Gloucester in 1724, they carry a total weight of 46½ cwt, and are still in working order, though 2 have been re-cast. Other interesting features in the church are a 12ft-long chest hewn from a single tree and bearing several old locks (theft from church is not something new), and an ornate Georgian font bearing the date 1722 and the name Thomas Bisse. The Reverend Dr Thomas Bisse has the distinction of being the first documented person to have preached at the world famous Three Choirs Festival at Hereford in 1720. This was one of the earliest services, and in 1724 he preached a momentous sermon at the event in Gloucester, when he asked that the collection should in future be given to charity, to the widows and orphans of the clergy – so began the tradition which still persists today.

CRADLEY

TYME TRYETH TROTH.

Near the church door and in the same well-tended grounds as the yew tree which boasts a certificate authenticating its 1200 years, these words adorn the sundial. One wonders what Queen Victoria might have thought had she known that this unusual inscription was being restored in June 1887 in celebration of her Diamond Jubilee. If 'troth' is taken to mean 'promise' (as in 'to plight one's troth'), Victoria was one lady who did not find time a trial in keeping her promise to her Consort.

To the south-east of the sundial is an interesting 15th-century timber-framed building. Formerly a boys' school, and now a busy and much used Parish Hall, there is a stone high in its rebuilt chimney stack which once recorded the work of two 17th-century church wardens, their names sadly now obliterated by time and weather.

TUPSLEY

A COCK HORSE.

Location: ½ mile from Hereford city centre on A438 to Ledbury.
Map Reference: O.S. map 149 (1:50,000); 535402

At a casual glance it would seem that the artist here has made a mistake, for clearly the illustration is not of a farm-yard cock. The name, however, is that given to the magnificent drey horses now rarely seen even in areas such as Herefordshire. A 'cock-horse' was kept ready at the foot of a steep hill to help a coach and its team to the top. In this case, the horses were stabled across the road from the inn at Tupsley, ready when necessary, to pull coaches and carts from Ledbury up the hill into Hereford.

MUNSLEY

HAMLET, PRINCE OF DENMARK?

Location: 4 miles north-west of Ledbury off the A438.
Map Reference: O.S. map 149 (1:50,000); 663410

This barely legible inscription can be found inside a small remote country church dating back to the Normans, and standing quietly on a slight rise above a willow-fringed duck pond, once a moat. In 1863 during restoration work in the Church of St Bartholomew, an ancient fragment of a sarcophagus was found. It bears the legend HAMLET XHETI (Hamlet the Jute) AD 362. Fixed to the south wall of the Nave, it is claimed to refer to the original Hamlet, Prince of Denmark, of Shakespeare's play. This story seems most unlikely but it is certainly a curious stone and the truth of its existence will never be known.

Photo: J.M.

MUNSLEY

A 'GREEN' ANGEL

On entering the churchyard, one is greeted by a topiary angel reading the Bible. It is a continuence of work begun by a local man who until the 1980s was famous for his topiary, creating in his garden tree like lions, birds, and even a jockey on a horse. It is to be hoped that this charming angel does not seccumb to neglect or to some arborial disease.

BOSBURY

A PLACE OF REFUGE.

Location: 5 miles north of Ledbury on the B4220.
Map Reference: O.S. map 149 (1:50,000); 695435

Standing firm and square, the 12th-century tower of the Church of The Holy Trinity dominates the quiet village of Bosbury. It is one of nine free-standing towers in Herefordshire and there are fewer than fifty in England. These were originally built as a fortified refuge from invaders who, until the 15th century, led attacks across the borders from Wales. Now Bosbury's tower, its spire removed in 1812, stands aloof and silent, brooding upon the hours which ring out from its clock.

Facing it, the Norman Church, still and spacious beneath its high timbered roof, houses some items of interest. In the Chancel are two heavily carved monuments to the 16th-century Harford family, while in the Morton chapel is a crumbling gravestone dated 1282, that of Stephen Swinfield whose son became Bishop of Hereford.

Photo: J.M.

29

BOSBURY

SAVED FROM THE PURITANS.

Between the church and its tower is a rare 14th-century Preaching Cross, rare because it is one of the few to escape destruction by Puritan fanatics. It survived only because in the 1650s the Reverend Wall, Vicar of Bosbury, pleaded with the Parliamentarians for its safety. They finally agreed it would be spared on condition that the following words were carved upon its arms:- 'Honour not the cross, but honour God for Christ'. Alas, these are no longer legible.

STOKE EDITH

A TRIPLE PULPIT.

Location: 6 miles from Hereford on the A438
Map Reference: O.S. map 149 (1:50,000); 604407

It is easy to pass through Stoke Edith en route to or from Hereford without knowing that a comparatively rare triple decker pulpit can be found in St Mary's Church. 'Triple Deckers' were made so that the Minister gave his sermon from the highest level, the service was conducted from the middle tier, while the Parish Clerk led the Responses from ground level. (See also Clodock and Shobdon).

The Church, rebuilt in the 18th century, is off the main road, tucked away beside Stoke Edith House, itself a relatively modern version of the original home of the great Foley family, burnt down in 1927, (though the octagonal west lodge on the A438 still catches the eye). The Church was originally dedicated to St Edith, a daughter of King Edgar, who became Abbess of Wilton in 976 AD when she was 15. Tradition tells us

Photo: J.M.

that one day workmen asked her for water, whereupon she prayed and at her feet a spring appeared. The grille over the well can still be seen beside the main gate to the house, and up to 100 years ago, so they say, people still bathed in its healing waters.

COLWALL

THE COLWALL STONE.

Location: 3 miles south west of Malvern on the B4218.
Map Reference: O.S. map 150 (1:50,000); 757425

The Colwall Stone, of sufficient note to be marked on some maps, is situated in the centre of the village sprawling on the western slopes of the Malverns. A large piece of limestone, it is the inspiration for several legends. Some say it was put there by the devil, others that it landed there after a giant living in a cave beneath the Herefordshire Beacon 3 miles away, threw it at his faithless wife and killed her. Yet others claim that it turns at midnight, but the more prosaic truth is that it was probably used as a huntsman's mounting block.

COLWALL

A CHURCH ALE HOUSE.

Location: 3 miles from Malvern and 1 mile down Mill Lane off B4218.
Map Reference: O.S. map 150 (1:50,000); 739423

The neat black and white building by the east gate of St James' Church is a Church Ale House. Thought to be 16th century, it is mentioned in an unpublished poem by one Jervis Markham, gent. 1600, now in the British Museum. He records that during a service at Maytime the parishioners went for a drink:

> *'Colwall, that towne on th'other syde the Hill,*
> *Such kyndnes shew'd me, I remember 't still . . . . . .*
> *About Mid-service, they goe in a Rowe*
> *After the Priest, into the Church-ale-house*
> *(Which in the churchyard standeth) to carouse.*
> *Not to carouse, say they, but breake their fast*
> *Because then Calves-heads will not longer last.*
> *Which being don, to church they hye agate*
> *Their latter service serves for after grate.' . . . . (sic).*

Gatherings in the Ale House were, in fact, equivalent to a church fete today. They flourished until the mid-17th century when Puritan disapproval caused Ale Houses to be used as schools or, as this one was, almeshouses. The Colwall building had been unoccupied since the 1930s, but was refurbished and re-opened by Viscountess Cobham in July 1990 for use as a church hall.

COLWALL

HOPE END.

Location: 2 miles north of Ledbury, through Wellington Heath off the B4214 to Bromyard.

Map Reference: O.S. map 149 (1:50,000); 723412

One would not expect to find a Moorish minaret in the Herefordshire countryside, but as a child Elizabeth Barrett Browning knew it well. This minaret was part of the building completed for Elizabeth's father Edward Moulton Barrett in 1815. The house where the young poet spent the early years of her life was demolished long ago, but the stable block has been lavishly refurbished and is now a peaceful country hotel. As well as the minaret, a solid Moorish gateway remains to remind one of Moulton Barrett's desire to build a house which would be unique in England.

LEDBURY

A PRIVATE RAILWAY STATION.

Location: ¹/₂ mile north of town centre on A417.
Map Reference: O.S. map 149 (1:50,000); 710387

Ledbury must have the only railway station in England where, during the summer, one may relax in a deck-chair, enjoying a cup of tea and a chat with the station master while waiting for the train. The station, the first in the West Midlands to be privately run, was opened in 1988 by transport consultant Gareth Davies by agreement with British Rail. Gareth is not, as one might expect, an avid train-spotter, but a transport historian deeply interested is the way the rail networks have been instrumental in changing the face of the country. He believes that a rural railway station should be an integral part of the community and he has an infinite faith in the future of rural railways. Anyone fuming in a traffic jam can only join him in his belief that one day an efficient train service will again be part of the social fabric of this country.

LEDBURY

A UNIQUE PAINTED ROOM.

Location: In Church Lane, above the Tourist Information Centre.
Map Reference: O.S. map 149 (1:50,000); 712376

Ledbury, a market town since the 12th century, has much that is well documented for the curiosity seeker – St Katherine's Hospital building (13th century), a mid-17th-century Market Hall, a church with Civil War bullets in its door and a free-standing tower, an old Grammar School, and links with both John Masefield and Elizabeth Barrett Browning. But it was in the upstairs room of No 1, Church Lane that, as recently as 1988, these unique 16th-century wall paintings were found. During restoration it was discovered that this intricate work had lain hidden for centuries beneath many layers of plaster, paint and paper. Over 400 years ago the paint had been applied directly to the original wattle and daub that infilled the timbers. At that time great houses boasted wall hangings of tapestry. Here, in the home of a townsman, it would appear that the hangings were imitated, painted on, along with suitable texts to elevate the mind. It is also of interest to discover that at least one of the inscriptions, copied about 1560, was taken from the Psalter printed in 1549. Clearly No. 1, Church Lane holds many more secrets which have yet to be unravelled. The Painted Room may be visited, but since it is reached by a narrow winding staircase, it is not easily accessible to the disabled.

16th-century inscription, Church Lane, Ledbury

FOWNHOPE

AND HOW MANY YARDS?

Location: 7 miles south-east of Hereford on the B4224. *Map Reference:* O.S. map 149 (1:50,000); 581343

Fownhope is a village that knows exactly where it stands, as this milestone shows. Behind it is one of its more striking buildings, St Mary's Church, once referred to as 'the little cathedral'. One of the largest churches in the County, it has grown through the centuries from a small Norman chapel to its present length of 119ft, and boasts a tall slender octagonal spire erected in the late 14th century and covered, so we are told, with 22,000 oak shingles.

Inside, an informative leaflet guides the interested visitor round, pointing out much besides the famous 12th-century tympanum which represents the church's patron saint, Mary. Outside the churchyard wall stocks remind us of one common method of punishment from past centuries, and not far from the church, Fownhope's history is represented in a more pictorial form.

St. Mary's Church, Fownhope

FOWNHOPE

FIVE HUNDRED YEARS, MAN AND BOY.

Trevor Makinson's unusual mural may be seen in the Restaurant of the timber framed Green Man Inn. Built in 1485, it was known for centuries as The Naked Boy, who, perched in a tree, here watches the characters who all came to the Inn in their time. Just entering on the left is one of Colonel Birch's 17th-century Roundheads, for Cromwell's troops rested here overnight on their way to Hereford after the siege of Goodrich; a judge and prisoner represent the years when the Inn served as a court and temporary prison; a coach and horses reminds us that this was once a coaching inn on the old main road between Hereford and Gloucester; and near the coach stands perhaps the most famous man of Fownhope, Tom Spring the boxer.

Once landlord of The Naked Boy, Tom Spring (real name Winter, 1795-1851), was England's Champion heavyweight boxer 1823-4. At that time a round lasted until one man was knocked down. His fight for the championship went for 77 bare fisted rounds and took 2 hours and 29 minutes. Spring was a popular man – in fact so many crammed on to the Grandstand at Worcester to witness one of his bouts that it collapsed under the weight. He is buried in West Norwood, London, but a local memorial was erected to him 100 years after his death by 'his countrymen of the land of cider in token of their esteem'. In the form of a cider mill-stone, it may be seen in a field off the road to Woolhope about 1 mile from Fownhope.

MUCH MARCLE

A MAN FROM CHAUCER'S ENGLAND.

Location: 7 miles north east of Ross off the A449, down a turning beside the
Walwyn Arms.
Map Reference: O.S. map 149 (1:50,000); 658328

Walter de Helyon lived in Much Marcle in the mid 14th century and this remarkable
wooden effigy brings him to life again more than 600 years after his death. Carved out of a
sold block of oak and 6ft 4 inches in length, it was once the lid of his stone sarcophagus,
but now lies on top of a 17th-century treble-locked chest in the peaceful Nave of St
Bartholomew's church. It is one of only two wooden monumental effigies in Herefordshire,
the other being at Clifford. There are fewer than 100 in England altogether, and this figure
was restored and repainted in 1972 while on loan to the London Museum for an exhibition
of Chaucer's London. Seeing Walter de Helyon cross-legged (unusual), resplendent in his
red buttoned tunic and complete with 'an anlaas and a gipser al of silk' (sic) (dagger and
purse) we have an idea of what Chaucer's Frankeleyn, or country gentleman, must have
looked like. It is said that until the late 19th century it was customary to carry this effigy at
the head of local funerals.

41

MUCH MARCLE

A NATURAL SHELTER.

Outside the church an ancient Yew tree has also been here for many centuries.It is so old and so large that its spreading branches are now supported by posts and timbers. In its 30ft hollow trunk there are seats for about 7 people who may sit and talk as they watch comings and goings through the church doorway. Yew is also clipped into delightful lych gates to the north and south of the building.

While in the area it is also worth looking at an historic house across from the church, called Hellens. Begun in 1292, it is one of the oldest homes in England still lived in by descendants of the family who built it. It may be visited on some afternoons between Easter and October.

One should also mention The Wonder, a natural pheno-menan 2¹/₂ miles north west of the church (149; 633365). A rockface, 15ft high, it is the result of a 3-day landslide in February 1575 when 'Marclay Hill . . . . roused itself out of a dead sleep and with a roaring noise removed from the place where it stood', destroying everything in its path.

SELLACK

GONE!

Location: 6 miles north-north west of Ross on a minor road off A49.
Map Reference: O.S. map 162 (1:50,000); 565276

The family of Elizabeth Dew were obviously people of few words. This succinct memorial to her life, with the single word just legible, stands in the churchyard to the east of St Tysilio's Church some distance from any main road.

The church itself is unique since it is the only one in England dedicated to the Celtic saint Tysilio, although there are others in Wales and Brittany, the most notable being at Llanfairpwllgwyngyllgogerychwyrndrobwllllantysiliogogogoch – which I am reliably informed means 'The Church of St Mary in a hollow of white hazel near to a rapid whirlpool and to St Tysilio's church near to a red cave'. Tysilio, whose Feast Day is 1st October, was born in Shrewsbury (then known as Pengwern), son of a King of Powys. Because he chose to forsake his inheritance in favour of a religious life, he was persecuted by his family and finally fled with his monks to Brittany. Here he founded a monastery and died about 650 AD.

SELLACK

A SUSPENSION BRIDGE.

Across the meadows behind the church one finds a suspension bridge across the River Wye – surely a curiosity since it is so incongruous in the midst of grazing cattle and willow trees. It was built in 1896 to replace a ford and ferry which originally provided a link between Sellack and Kings Caple. Paid for by public subscription and having a span of 190ft, it is one of two such bridges across the Wye, the other being at Foy. One hopes that it will remain for many years to come, for it is certainly a more pleasant way of passing from one village to the other than driving along the highway.

ROSS-ON-WYE

A PHILANTHROPIST'S TOWN.

This bustling market town set on a sandstone cliff above the Wye has many things of interest for the curiosity seeker. Most know of the Market Hall standing proudly on a rise in the centre of the town. Probably built between 1660 and 1674 at the instigation of Frances, wife of the 2nd Duke of Somerset, it stands before number 34, another notable building, once home of philanthropist John Kyrle (1637-1734), Pope's 'Man of Ross'.

The Market Hall, Ross-on-Wye

ROSS-ON-WYE

A PHILANTHROPIST'S TOWN.

Born in Dymock and a man of law, though he never practiced, Kyrle was not only a philanthropist, he was also a Royalist. Opposite his window on the south wall of the Market Hall he had carved a medallion, the FC and heart meaning 'Faithful to Charles (II) in heart'. Kyrle was an enthusiastic architect, builder and gardener. He spent much of his wealth improving the area by town planning and social welfare. Among many other things, he was responsible for the town's first water supply, the Prospect public gardens with its tower on the North side (opposite the Royal Hotel), and the pinnacle of the church tower. This he doubtless admired as he sat at the door of his unusual gothic summerhouse, looking out on his own private tree shaded knot garden.

ROSS-ON-WYE

A SWAN MOSAIC.

It is here at the back of Kyrle's house that one finds a true 'curiosity'. At the foot of three steps leading from the door of the summerhouse is a swan mosaic made of horses' teeth. It is said that the teeth came from horses killed in a cavalry battle at Witton Bridge during the Civil War. Kyrle paid money for every tooth brought to him. The surface of each one, which is what one sees, looks like a pebble, but on examining a loose one, there is no doubt that it is, in fact, a full length tooth. At time of writing, the summerhouse, which was allowed to fall into disrepair, is not open to the public; but happily it is now being carefully restored by its new owner so that one day we may again enjoy the tranquillity of Kyrle's own garden. Here it may be fitting to remember that it was through a member of the Kyrle Society (founded 1877), a lady named Octavia Hill, that the National Trust was formed – so in an oblique way Kyrle's 'green' influence remains very much alive.

ROSS-ON-WYE

ST. MARY'S CHURCH.

Kyrle lay in state for nine days after his death and is buried in the sanctuary of St. Mary's Church a short distance from his home. Here, apart from his monument, is yet another memorial to him, a most fitting one which he, who planted so many trees, would have appreciated. The creepers growing up before a window replace two Elms which began to grow some years after his death close to the pew where Kyrle always sat. They remained there until they, too, died and had to be removed. Now, to maintain the tradition, these new plants are based in a stone trough and are carefully nurtured to grow like the original trees, which came either from shoots from the elms Kyrle planted in the churchyard or perhaps from seeds which dropped from his own pocket.

The church itself is rich in monuments, not least those to the Rudhall family who built the picturesque Almshouses in Church St., and the organ chamber which was given by a Miss Sarah Hall who, until a year before her death at the age of 105, walked to church every Sunday from her home 1/4 mile away.

ROSS-ON-WYE

A PLAGUE CROSS.

Outside St. Mary's, in the grounds bordering on Church St. is a rare Plague Cross. It has been restored but the inscription on its base causes one to pause. It illustrates the horrors inflicted by plagues which in the past swept through communities so swiftly that whole families were wiped out. In this case 1 in 3 of the population succumbed. Standing near the pit into which bodies were thrown, it reads:

'Plague Ano Dom 1637,
Burials 323 Libera Nos Domine.'

One can only be thankful for modern medicine.

ROSS-ON-WYE

'AND DO NOT MAKE DELAY'.

In the middle recess of Wilton Bridge is this tall 18-century sundial. Modern traffic is considerably heavier than when the bridge was built (1597-9) or the sundial set in place, so that anyone wishing to read the barely legible inscription must take care when crossing, and heed its message – although originally the warning was perhaps against wasting time gazing into the peaceful water below:

Esteem thy precious time
Which pass so swift away,
Prepare thee for eternity
And do not make delay.

It is said that the recesses on the bridge – the originals on one side were lost through road widening – were used by traders at the time of plague in 1637. Here they left their goods rather than enter the town and risk infection. Payment was left in like manner, any coins standing in bowls of vinegar which acted as a disinfectant.

BROCKHAMPTON-BY-ROSS

A THATCHED CHURCH.

Location: 5 miles north of Ross, west of the B4224.
Map Reference: O.S. map 149 (1:50,000); 594321

The unusual partly thatched church of All Saints has taken over from the now ruined Medieval Church of The Holy Trinity in the grounds of Brockhampton Court. It is known as an 'Arts and Crafts' church because the architect, W.R. Lethaby (1857-1931), went to such pains to echo medieval design and age-old craftsmanship in its relatively modern construction. Built in 1901 by Alice Foster of Brockhampton Court in memory of her parents, Eben and Julia Jordan of Boston, Massachusetts U.S.A., it shows us the work of the best sculptors, artists, weavers, carpenters and wood-carvers, and the oak they used was all Herefordshire grown. Famous craftsmen such as William Morris, Burne Jones and Christopher Whall were all in some way represented here, so that the whole becomes a most impressive piece of early 20th-century architecture.

Mounted on the wall is an earlier example of church craftsmanship, a 16th-century triptych, partly Flemish, its paintings as alive now as when they were first created.

This beauty is somewhat marred as one returns to the road through the thatched lychgate. Opposite, the gatehouse to the Court (now a hotel), boasts an incongruous bright red Post Office sign on its lovely timbered walls. It's a pity this 20th-century cipher has to intrude so harshly.

WESTON UNDER PENYARD

'FOR THEE I WOULD A CASTLE MAKE. . .'

Location: 14 miles south of Hereford on a minor road linking A40 and B4224.
Map Reference: O.S. map 162 (1:50,000); 638238

Just to the north of the village lie these buildings which appear to be those of a castle. In fact they are a sham, and are 17th-century barns converted during the following century by a husband who, it is said, wished to please his wife. The barns lie behind a house built in Stuart times on the site of an old Roman settlement. Legend has it that a new bride wished to live in a castle and so her husband added an assortment of out-buildings embellished with battlements and turrets and a moat. History doesn't tell us whether the lady was pleased, but at least we may enjoy the eccentricity of Bollitree Castle as we pass through the village.

LITTLE BIRCH

HIGGINS' WELL.

Location: 6 miles south of Hereford, off the A49 Hereford to Ross road.
Map Reference: O.S. map 149 (1:50,000); 512313

Higgins' Well, in the middle of a field in a dip behind the church, is not easy to find, although doubtless the animals that welcome its waters have never had any trouble locating it. It began years ago as a natural spring on the land of one Mr. Higgins. At first he took exception to people and animals coming on to his land for water and he closed off the supply at a higher level. Then one evening, so the story goes, he was sitting beside his fireside when suddenly his feet were immersed in water which seemed to come from nowhere. He realised then the mistake he had made, and to pacify the spirit of the waters he re-opened the well. Said to flow even in drought, and with water which looks very pure and clear, it has two levels – one for people and one for animals. The well is in its present good condition because it was restored and enlarged by public subscription, at the instigation of H.W. Southey JP, to commemorate the Diamond Jubilee of Queen Victoria in 1897.

HOARWITHY

AN UNEXPECTED ITALIANATE CHURCH

> *Location:* 9 miles south-south-east of Hereford along A49 to Ross, turning off left about 1¹/₂ miles after Much Birch and then along minor road.
> *Map Reference:* O.S. map 149 (1:50,000); 546294

St Catherine's must be the most unexpected church in Herefordshire. Standing on a rise above the village, it looks with its open cloister, as if it has been transported from Italy. It encases the original chapel which was built here in 1840, a building described by William Poole, later vicar of the parish, as 'an ugly brick building with no pretensions to any style of architecture'. In 1870 he decided to use his own money to do something about the church he so disliked. With his friend, the architect Seddon, he added to the chapel, copying designs from France, Venice and Italy, and importing both craftsmen and materials. The result is this Italianate church, a popular place for visitors who come to enjoy not only the views, but the church's lovely internal features – carved saints, painted tie beams, white marble altar inlaid with Lapis Lazuli and Tiger Eye, and floor mosaics which lead through the nave from the Cloister where, in mosaic, one is bidden to 'Keep they foot when thou goest to the house of God'.

HENTLAND

THE STORY OF ST. DUBRICIUS

> *Location:* 2 miles from Hoarwithy, passing the New Harp Inn in the direction of Ross and taking a side road to the right, then down a narrow track.
> *Map Reference:* O.S. map 162 (1:50,000); 543264

2 miles from St Catherine's and in the same parish, Hentland church is one of several dedicated to the 5th century priest St Dubricius. His picture, complete with hedgehog (once the County's symbol) and the date AD470 appears in a window in the north wall. He was a man about whom there is an interesting legend. It is thought he was born at Madley, the son of Eurdil who was the daughter of Peibau, the King of Archenfield. For many years Peibau had suffered from an unfortunate condition which caused him to foam at the mouth, so that he was known as King Dribbler. Before his grandson was born, Peibau on finding that Eurdil was pregnant, ordered that she be drowned in the River Wye. Each time they tried to carry out the sentence she saved herself. The king then ordered that she be burnt alive, but on returning to Madley the next morning his servants found Eurdil sitting by the ashes with her new-born baby, Dubricius. On seeing them, the king softened. As Peibau bent toward his daughter, the child touched his grandfather's face, and from then on, the legend says, the king was cured of his unfortunate malady and dribbled no more.

Dubricius is believed to have founded a College for priests in this area, one which attracted more then 2,000 clerics to its doors before he moved it to Moccas. Dubricius finally retired to Bardsey where he lived a solitary life until his death in 612 AD.

PEACE AND GOOD NEIGHBOURHOOD

Historically the church at Hentland is interesting for two other reasons. The yew tree by the lane gate is known to have been planted on Shrove Tuesday, 13th February in 1615, for it is so recorded in the parish records. St Dubricius is also famous for being one of only three parish churches which still distribute Pax Cakes to the congregation on Palm Sunday each year, (the others being at Kings Caple and Sellack). Each year the small biscuits are made by a local baker to a traditional design – the Lamb of God in the centre edged by the legend Peace and Good Neighbourhood. The custom is rooted in Medieval times, but was

perpetuated in the 16th century by a 5/-bequest from the Scudamore family in an effort to stamp out family feuds which had continued through the centuries. Currently paid for by charities, the words are now perhaps even more relevant as a message for Holy Week.

LLANGORRAN

SUNDIAL ON A STEEPLE.

Location: 14 miles south of Hereford, 3 miles from St Weonards, off B4251.
Map Reference: O.S. map 162 (1:50,000); 530211

A sundial set on the tip of a church spire is certainly unique, something to be sought out by any curiosity seeker. How could one read a sundial set so high? But all is not what one imagines. At the church of St Deinst the spire has been brought down to earth. During restoration the tip of the steeple was replaced and the old stones set in the churchyard as the sundial's base.

The church, which dates back to the 14th century is one of only two dedicated to St Deinst, the other being at Itton in Monmouthshire, but little is known of him and he does not figure in the dictionary of saints.

ST WEONARDS

WHO WAS ST WEONARD?

> *Location:* 11 miles south of Hereford on the A466 to Monmouth.
> *Map Reference:* O.S. map 162 (1:50,000); 496243

The church here is unique in being the only one which records this Celtic saint. No-one is really sure who he was, although tradition has it that he was a hermit and a woodcutter. It is thought he may have had some connection with Dubricious who died in 550 (see Hentland), and it is recorded that at one time he was represented in a stained glass window in the chancel of this church. In 1670 someone described the figure as being of 'an old man in Hermit's array' holding a book in one hand and an axe in the other, adding 'the remaynes of writing is only Wenardus Heremita' (sic). The window has long gone and there is no known feast day to this almost unknown monastic saint, so the mystery remains.

GARWAY

BROTHER RICHARD'S COLUMBARIUM.

> *Location:*   5 miles south-east of Pontrilas on the B4347 Monmouth to Pontrilas road
> ³/₄ mile from The Moon pub on Garway common.
> *Map Reference:* O.S. map 161 (1:50,000); 455224

This dovecote, the oldest in the County, is in the private grounds of Church Farm. It stands, hugging its history to itself, while clucking hens scratch busily at its feet. Built in 1326, vaulted, with walls 4ft thick, and nesting places for 666 birds set in 19 rows, it once bore an inscription above its door – 'Brother Richard built this columbarium.' Sadly the weather has practically destroyed this reference to Brother Richard, but the shape of the dovecote reminds us of the church to which it is historically linked.

The church of St Michael and All Angels, one of six churches of the Knights Templar, stands to the north of its dovecote. The circular foundations of the original 12th century Nave (round because it was the shape of the church of the Holy Sepulchre in Jerusalem), may be seen on the north side of the later church building.

GOODRICH

A NOBLE CASTLE.

Location: 5 miles south-south-west of Ross off A40.
Map Reference: O.S. map 162 (1:50,000); 577200

The entrance to Goodrich Castle, although imposing, can only suggest the strength of its sturdy foundations. Rising out of the red sandstone on which it stands, the mainly 13th-century building exudes a feeling of power and permanence. On a natural spur 100 ft above the south bank of the Wye and rebuilt on the site of a Norman earthwork castle, this 'noblest ruin in Herefordshire' has been included as a representative of the many castles which once guarded the borders into Wales. An excellent guide-book produced by English Heritage gives full information on this masterpiece of defensive building. Since Civil War battles in 1646 it has stood empty, but still proud. Naturally, a castle has its legends. One tells of two lovers who took shelter here during the Civil War. It was in the hands of Royalists then but was besieged by Colonel Birch and his Roundheads (he who later rested at Fownhope). The lovers tried to escape across the river but were drowned and are now said to haunt the Wye, their ghosts crossing on a phantom horse. Ironically, the girl was Alice Birch, the Colonel's niece – such is the pain of war.

GOODRICH

THE CROSS COTTAGE.

Near the road leading to the Castle one may drink at 'Ye Olde Hostelrie'. Unlike its neighbour, it is not as old as it appears. It was built in 1830, its pinnacles and gothic windows being copied from an old illumination in an effort to maintain the history of the area. Beside it, however, is The Cross, a genuine historical building which has stood for more than 400 years. Before the Dissolution it is believed to have been a chapel and a resting place for pilgrims, for it stands on an old track which once led to Tintern Abbey. Above the front door is a small crest showing 11 creatures which have been called herons, but which are not really so clearly defined. Now a private house, it may not be explored, but one wonders what stories the stones could tell if only they could speak.

GOODRICH

J.B. HERBERT AND THOMAS SWIFT.

> *Location:* ³/₄ mile south of the Castle off B4229.
> *Map Reference:* O.S. map 162 (1:50,000); 572190

High on a hill in the churchyard of St Giles lies this boulder, a memorial to 3 members of the Herbert family who all 'fell asleep' in 1863, '64 and '72 respectively. It is said that Mr. Herbert (presumably J.B. who died in 1863) was a church warden who specifically asked for this form of gravestone – the reason why is not recorded. The boulder was brought from the foot of Doward Hill by a traction engine and part of the wall had to be removed before it could be manoeuvred into the churchyard. One wonders if the inscription beneath his name was decided after his death by the family as a wry comment, for it reads 'Let not the strong man Glory in his strength'. No epitaph is added to the later inscriptions.

One of the church's more famous rectors was 17th century Thomas Swift, Dean Swift's grandfather, now buried beneath the altar. He was a staunch Royalist who, it is said, forgot his Christian tenets so far as to have spiked iron balls laid in the river in an attempt to lame Parliamentary horses. Later, after the battle of Naseby, he made a gift of a waistcoat to his King, Charles I – a rich gift indeed, for in the lining were secreted 300 very acceptable gold sovereigns. The church is locked but a key may be obtained from the Vicarage nearby.

SYMONDS YAT

A-MAZING.

Location: 6 miles south west of Ross on Wye off the A40 to Monmouth.
Map Reference: O.S. map 162 (1:50,000); 556175; (Cave: 546156)

In the Jubilee Park at Symonds Yat the recently created and popular Maze is found beside the only permanent Maze Museum in the world. The Maze, planted by Lindsay and Edward Heyes in 1977 to celebrate the Queen's Silver Jubilee, is one of only two designed in the 'labyrinth of love' style, the other being at Hanover. The unique Museum is a fascinating 'hands on' experience. Visitors are invited to trace historical mazes and labyrinths (do you know the difference?), while learning about their history and meaning – whether they have magical origins or are just puzzles for enjoyment. The exhibition also looks into the future and challenges you to beat a maze-solving robot.

While in this area, it is worth searching out King Arthur's Cave on nearby Doward Hill near Whitchurch. It is said that Arthur hid here while fleeing from the Saxons but it is more famous for the discovery of Stone Age flints and the bones of animals which once roamed free – woolly rhinocerous, mammoth, reindeer, bison and hyena. Across from the cave is the Suckstone, at 60ft long said to be the largest boulder in Britain, and possibly a marker on a ley-line through from the cave to the Buckstone, another boulder across the county border on a ridge near Staunton.

BACTON

A QUEEN'S MAID.

> *Location:* 1 mile north of Abbey Dore off the B4347.
> *Map Reference:* O.S. map 149 (1:50,000); 371323

The 13th-century church of St Faith at Bacton is yet another example of a small unassuming country church which hides a treasure. The monument to Blanche Parry and her royal mistress is set in the chancel beneath a lovely Tudor roof and a row of carved angels bearing shields. The monument is rare in that it is one of the few known effigies of Queen Elizabeth I carved in her lifetime. Blanche, born in peaceful Bacton, obviously never forgot her roots even though her life changed so dramatically. She was 28 when she first became a Lady in Waiting to the 3-year-old Princess Elizabeth and she served her royal mistress faithfully all her life until, as Chief Gentlewoman of the Privy Chamber, she died in her 81st year. By then, having witnessed all the drama and intrigue of court life, she must have known the Queen better than anyone – there must be many historians who would have welcomed her autobiography. Blanche was buried at Westminster but her heart, it is said, is buried beneath this monument. She bequeathed £500 to Bacton so that almshouses could be built, along with 20 cows for the use of local people who were expected to pay 2/- a year to the vicar for the use of each cow. Here she is seen kneeling beside the somewhat stunted figure of her Queen, while the long inscription ends with the information that she, 'never no mans wyffe . . . . wythe maeden quene a maede dyd ende . . . (her) . . . lyffe'. (sic)

Some say that the silk embroidered altar cloth in a glass case in the Nave is Blanche's handiwork. Whether it is or not, it is an exquisite piece of workmanship, nearly as beautiful now as it was when it was made almost 400 years ago.

ABBEY DORE

FINE RENAISSANCE WOODWORK.

> *Location:* 13 miles south-west of Hereford, 2 miles north of Pontrilas on B4347.
> *Map Reference:* O.S. map 149 (1:50,000); 388304

This beautiful oak screen is another example of the work of John Abel, the King's Carpenter, who was also responsible here for the oak pulpit, the pews, sidescreens and the lovely ceiling. The screen is part of restoration work carried out by Viscount Scudamore 1633-34. He restored the remains of the old Abbey Church, originally built in 1180 by Cistercian Monks whose way of life was one of simplicity and purity. The latin words on the screen frieze * are exactly the same as the first 2 lines of the verse decorating the Market House at Leominster, also built by Abel in the same year. Abbey Dore on the bank of the river derives from the Welsh 'dour' meaning water – therefore 'the abbey by the stream'.

* *'Vive deo gratus toti mundo tumulatus crimine mundatus semper transire paratus'.*
  'Live in a way pleasing to God entirely buried as regards the world, free from reproach, always ready to pass from hence'.

ABBEY DORE

THE GRIM REAPER.

This representation of a rather muscular Angel of Death, complete with flowing cloak and scythe, is one of the paintings decorating the Abbey walls. This, along with other figures, patterns and Biblical texts, were painted at the time of the 17-century restoration.

KILPECK

A NORMAN LEGACY.

Location: 8 miles from Hereford, south of the A465 to Abergavenny.
Map Reference: O.S. map 149 (1:50,000); 444305

Photo CH.

Few need to be told of the Church of St Mary and St David at Kilpeck, for it is reputed to be the most perfect example of Norman architecture in Britain. It was built in 1135 AD by the Benedictines of St Peter who founded a Priory here, and was restored in 1848. The rich, beautifully preserved carvings have been much photographed, especially the south doorway with its Tree of Life on the tympanum. Here we see detail of some of the strange but beautifully executed figures above the right shaft of the door. In all more than 70 carvings are left even though, during the careful restoration it is said, a few were removed by the Victorian restorers, who considered that they were too erotic in detail to be renewed.

CLODOCK

TO A WELSH SAINT.

> *Location:*   12 miles south east of Hay on Wye, on minor road off B4347.
> *Map Reference:* O.S. map 161 (1:50,000); 326275

The parish church of St Clydawg in Clodock on the south-west border of the county is unique in being the only one of this dedication in the world. Clydawg was a 6th century King of Ewias greatly admired for his Christian virtues, who while out hunting, was killed by a rival for the hand of a lady. When his funeral procession reached the River Monnow, the oxen pulling his bier refused to cross the ford and the yoke joining them to the cart snapped. To Clydawg's followers this was a holy sign, so he was buried beside the river. In the years following his murder, Clydawg became a martyr. An enclosure was created round his tomb and people gathered to worship with him as they had during his life. November 3rd was regarded as his Saints Day, and in time the church and village came in to being here in the shadow of the Black Mountains. Until the time of Henry VIII the parish was part of Wales, and the church only came under the Diocese of Hereford in 1858.

The church itself is an historic gem, with its fine triple pulpit, Musician's Gallery, boxed pews and early wall paintings.

ROWLESTONE

CHAUNTICLEER AND PERTELOTE.

Location: 6 miles south-west of Kilpeck, 4 miles east of Clodock, on minor road off
            A465.
Map Reference: O.S. map 161 (1:50,000); 374271

These candelabra in the church of St Peter are among the rarest pieces of wrought-iron work in Britain. Made about 1500, they are approximately 55 inches long and hinged to fold back against the wall on either side of the chancel. They are each designed to hold 5 long candles and depict on one cocks, and on the other hens (or doves?), alternating with gilded fleur-de-lis.

On entering the 12th-century church, one is bidden to 'Look for the Tympanum' above the door, where, in the picture of Christ in Majesty, one sees a good example of the carver's art, not unlike that at Shobdon. The curiosity seeker may also wonder at the carving of St Paul in the chancel arch. Why is he upside down?

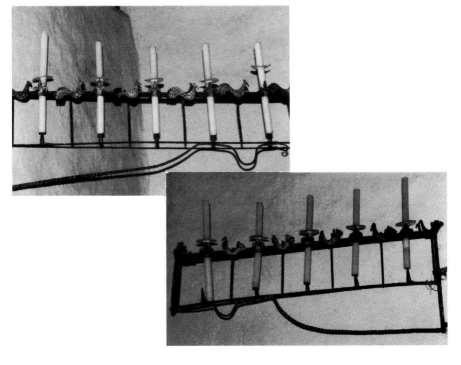

Chancel arch, St. Peter's Church.

DORSTONE

WHAT TIME IS IT?

> *Location:* 15 miles west of Hereford on B4348.
> *Map Reference:* O.S. map 148 (1:50,000); 314418

If the base of this sundial looks clumsy and out of proportion to the 'sun clock' above it, it is because until 1812 the stone was once part of the old village cross. The dial itself is unusual in having equidistant hour spacing, the figures clearly marked, with 11 being at the 'twenty-five past' point. It is believed to be slanted at this angle so as to be parallel with the Equator.

On one side of the sundial is the old Pandy Inn, built at the end of the 12th century and listing Cromwell as one of its guests, while on the other lies Dorstone church. Tradition has it that a chapel was founded here in expiation of his crime by Richard de Brito, one of the three knights who murdered Thomas a Becket. The present church dates from 1890, and at that time part of a stone was found bearing an inscription and the date 1256, and a tomb equally old, containing still perfect bones and a tiny pewter coffin chalice. So it would appear that tradition could well be founded on fact.

DORSTONE

THOR'S STONE?

> *Location:* 1½ miles from Dorstone village, on a hill summit off the B4348 Hay to Peterchurch Road.
>
> *Map Reference:* O.S. map 148 (1:50,000); 318431

High on Meerbach Hill we find a Neolithic tomb which would once have been buried beneath a mound of earth. Vertical stones line the burial chamber and are topped by a great slab (now broken in two) which is 2ft thick, nearly 20ft long, graduating in width from 3ft to 11ft, and estimated to weigh about 25 tons. One can only wonder at the strength and persistence of our ancestors in placing it there 5000 years ago. Such a remarkable artefact, now maintained by English Heritage, has naturally given rise to myth and legend. Was the God Thor worshiped here, thus giving it its name Thor's stone – Dorstone – and was it once a sacrificial stone of the ancient Druids? Was it a landmark on which 3 Leylines centred? Did King Arthur know of its existence? Whatever its history, Arthur's Stone, as it is officially known, is a remarkable reminder of times past.

BREDWARDINE

'HE BEING DEAD YET SPEAKETH'.

Location: 12 miles north west of Hereford off the A438 to Hay-on-Wye.
Map Reference: O.S. map 149 (1:50,000); 335445

The tiny village of Bredwardine has become known to people all over the world through

the Diaries of the Victorian clergyman, Francis Kilvert. Visitors to the Church of St Andrew high above the western bank of the River Wye may rest on a stone seat to his memory. It faces the hills he loved and is found beneath an ancient Yew which now leans towards his grave on the north side of the church as if pointing to it. Here in 1879, at 38 still only a young man, and 10 days after his wedding, the Reverend Francis Kilvert was buried after a short illness. Born near Chippenham in Wiltshire, he had become Vicar of Bredwardine in 1877. During the years of his Diaries, 1870-79, he recorded not only his love of the countryside and its people, but also many aspects of Victorian social history. Those wishing to explore Kilvert's Bredwardine will enjoy a short tour of the area organised by the Kilvert Society which was formed in 1948. Leaflets detailing the walk may be found in the church.

BREDWARDINE

NORMAN ARTWORK

The Church of St Andew itself is 11th century with later additions, although its parish registers date only from 1723. Here one finds a large Norman font (nearly 4ft in diameter) hewn from a single rock, and beside the north doorway also Norman and now blocked up, a list of Vicars since 1277. On the external lintel of this low doorway and clearly seen from the churchyard near Kilvert's memorial, are curious old carvings of what appear to be a monkey and a bird.

WHITNEY-ON-WYE

HOW MUCH TO CROSS?

> *Location:* 16 miles from Hereford, 4 from Hay on Wye on the A438.
> *Map Reference:* O.S. map 148 (1:50,000); 258474

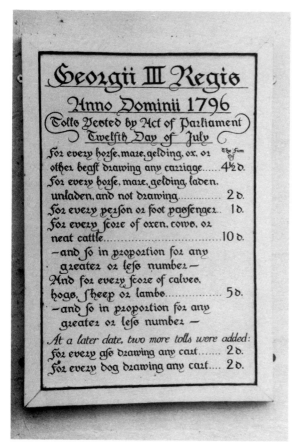

Two hundred years ago it cost 4½d (about 2p) to cross the Whitney Toll Bridge in a carriage. Today it costs 50p for a car – or a tractor. The charge for 'neat cattle' is not now advertised. Old toll bridges are rare today, but this one still used at Whitney is valuable enough to receive a Grade 2 listing. A bridge here over the Wye was first suggested in 1774, and between that year and 1795 three were built but, in spite of their 5 stone arches, all were washed away by floods. In 1796 Parliament proposed this 4th bridge. This time the 3 centre arches were made of timber noted for its durability and so the bridge still stands firm. It was privately funded and remained in the same family for nearly 200 years. Its current owners took over in 1990.

RHYDSPENCE INN

THE LAST INN IN ENGLAND.

Location: On the A438 on the Welsh border, 4 miles north of Hay on Wye.
Map Reference: O.S. map 148 (1:50,000); 244472

The lovely black and white Rhydspence Inn sits right on the border between England and Wales at the foot of Drovers Lane which comes down from the Brilley Uplands. The door in the photograph was once the front entrance, but because of re-alignment of the roads it is now to the rear of the building. Dating from about 1350, this was once a Drovers Inn, and it is possible to see quite clearly, in the left hand wall of the room above the porch, a peep-hole about 4 inches square. This looks out of what was once the Head Drovers' Room. It was from here that the men could keep watch for the herds of cattle as they came south to market at Hay-on-Wye, while at the same time enjoying a rest and a drink.

MANSELL LACEY

'...AND DOVES UPSTAIRS'

Location: 7 miles north-north-west of Hereford off A480.
Map Reference: O.S. map 149 (1:50,000); 425456

This pretty cottage, built in 1680 and standing near the church, has in its time had hundreds of people pass through its door. For years it was the village post office (a Victorian post box is in the wall beside it), and the dove cote above made it unique. Now it is a private house, but sensitive conversion has retained the original features. The 300-year old-dove cote has become a pretty bedroom, but externally its appearance is the same. The post office beneath was separated from a small apple store to the rear by old beams and wattle of hazel and ash, and these, too, are still in place. It is nice to know that although we may only admire it from the outside now, Ivy Cottage, complete with its 17th-century features, is well cared for and appreciated by its 20th-century owners.

KINNERSLEY

HOME IS A CASTLE.

Location: 12 miles south-west of Leominster on the A4112 to Brecon.
Map Reference: O.S. map 149 (1:50,000); 345496

It is most unusual in this area to see crow-stepped brick gables such as are on Kinnersley Castle. Crow stepped gables are usually associated with Jacobean work, and since the house is Elizabethan, they must be an extremely rare and early example of this particular design. Originally a Welsh border castle, the house was reconstructed in the late 16th century, and still retains its leaded window panes, fine oak panelled walls and beautiful Elizabethan plaster work. Pevsner, the great authority on historical architecture, was very interested in the timber arches when he visited the Castle. They are let into the walls, two in the hall and one on the first floor, and he said this was something he had never seen before in a house such as this. Although a family home, it is possible to view the house and gardens at certain times during the summer, and it is available for conferences throughout the year.

EARDISLEY

A MAGNIFICENT FONT.

Location: 16 miles south-west of Leominster on the A4111 to Kington.
Map Reference: O.S. map 148 (1:50,000); 312491

This beautiful font in the Church of St Mary Magdalene dates back to the middle of the 12th century and shows some of the outstanding work of the Herefordshire School of Carvers. (see also Castle Frome). The lion , with one eye closed and the other open, is rendered harmless by the Celtic plaitwork above and below him, while the carving on the dress of the soldiers is meticulously executed and incorporates pre-Conquest design.

Eardisley village itself is steeped in history. Noted in the Domesday Book as Herdeslege, and surrounded by woods, it has many houses dating back to the 17th and 18th centuries and earlier. Castle Farm, for example, stands on the site of the old Castle Eardisley, one of Domesday's two 'domus defensabiles', the earliest defensive houses in England (and they were both in Herefordshire). The Tram Inn, which can be recommended for its hospitality, is 16th century and a reminder that Eardisley was also once on the now disused Kington-Brecon tramway. A short way up the lane beside the Inn (sign posted Woodseaves) is the Eardisley Oak, large enough to shelter 6 in its hollow 30ft circumference trunk.

KINGTON

WHERE 'EAGLES' FLY.

Location: 13 miles west of Leominster, 1¹/₂ miles north west of Kington off A44.
Map Reference: O.S. map 148 (1:50,000); 285581

This north-west corner near the county's border can boast of having the highest 18-hole golf course in England. Here, at the top of Bradnor Hill and 1284ft above sea level, golfers may relax in the Club House after enjoying unspoilt panoramic views while they play. Since it is set at the end of a narrow climbing road, only occasional visitors to this `National Trust land share the area with contented sheep and those fortunate enough to play on this course.

PEMBRIDGE

MEDIEVAL MARKET PLACE.

Location: 7 miles west of Leominster on the A44 to Kington.
Map Reference: O.S. map 149 (1:50,000); 391581

Standing below a lovely black and white coaching house called the New Inn (new, that is, before Tudor times), is the old early 17th-century Market Hall for Pembridge. The original mark stone can still be seen on the east side, and this was the place where for centuries people had gathered to exchange goods, and from which the word 'market' comes. Pembridge was granted its own market as far back as 1240. It is also possible to see the base of an old medieval cross on which the north-east pillar stands, and notches in the oak pillars themselves where traders fixed the planks on which they set out their wares.

PEMBRIDGE

PAGODA OR BELL TOWER?

Adjacent to the Market Square is this unusual 3-storey bell tower. One of only 7 in Herefordshire detached from its church, it is thought that it was erected while the church was being built, as a framework to support the bells and subsequently left when the church tower failed to materialise. Standing beside the gracious 14th-century church of St Mary, it is 48ft in diameter, a solid structure of stone and timber. Inside one can easily believe it was used as a place of refuge in times of strife, for the walls are nearly 2ft thick. The beams, still bearing the shape of the trees from which they were cut, are secured with traditional wooden pegs, and the whole building may truly be said to be unique.

SHOBDON

A 'GOTHIC' INTERIOR.

Location: 8 miles north-west of Leominster, 11/2 miles from Mortimers Cross off the B4362. *Map Reference:* O.S. map 149 (1:50,000); 401628. (Arches 401632).

One of the more striking aspects of the church of St John the Evangelist at Shobdon is the choice of blue and white for all interior decoration, from the ceilings to the pews and the triple decker pulpit It was rebuilt on the site of a Norman church by Viscount Bateman of Shobdon Court, Treasurer of the Royal Household of George II, and completed in 1756. The architect is believed to have been Richard Bentley (1708-1782), known as 'the Gothickist', a man renowned for this particular style of 'Rococo Gothic' architecture.

SHOBDON

ARCHES OF TIME.

In an act of conservation some of the remains of the original Norman church were re-erected in the grounds of Shobdon Park ¼ mile away. The Arches, as they are known, form a striking 'eye catcher' on a rise at the end of a tree-lined avenue, and consist of the old chancel arch and two doorways. Conservation partly failed, however, because the original carvings on the tympanum have been badly eroded by weather. One can only hope that the arches themselves will stand for many years to come, since in appearance, they are the nearest thing to a folly that Herefordshire has.

WIGMORE

EDUCATION 17th-CENTURY STYLE.

Location: 21 miles north-north west of Hereford on the A4110.
Map Reference: O.S. map 148 (1:50,000); 413691

This village in the north of the county was once the medieval home of the Mortimer family, for centuries rulers of the Welsh Marches. It was the setting for a castle, an abbey and the beginnings of education. The castle, seat of the Mortimers, originally built by King Alfred's daughter and fortified by the Normans, has long gone; the abbey now forms the basis of Wigmore Grange, but the 17th-century school-house remains. Now a private dwelling, it was founded in May 1659 by one William Allen, a yeoman, who willed that there should be here a house for 'one honest maid or single woman therein, that can teach children to sewe and reade and shee to have the same rent free as long as shee behaveth herselfe well'. Modern children, enjoying a more varied curriculum, are now served by a large modern school on the outskirts of Wigmore.

While here, it is worth looking at the Church of St James which looms above the old school house. It appears large for so small a village until one remembers the area's historic importance. Its near circular churchyard on a ridge surrounded by a wall, suggests a large Celtic foundation to the Norman and 14th-century building. Here, beneath the altar, we are told, lies the tomb of a reverend gentleman who was wise and astute enough to live through the many vicissitudes of 17th-century religious strife. During his 51 years as minister for Wigmore, from the time of Charles I through to William and Mary, the

Reverend Alexander Clogie swayed through the changes from High Church to Puritanism and back again until he died in October 1698, aged 84, hoping for 'glorious resurrection unto life eternall' – something his flexibility had surely earned.

BIBLIOGRAPHY

Andere M., *Herefordshire, The Enchanted Land.*

Andere M., *Homes and Houses of Herefordshire.*

A. A., *Beautiful Britain Series – Heart of England.*

Baker and Morris, *The Middle Marches.*

County Council Register, *Herefordshire Countryside Treasures, 1981.*

Haines G.H., *Shropshire and Herefordshire Villages.*

Herefordshire Federation of W.I., *The Herefordshire Village Book.*

Herefordshire Historic Churches Trust, *Discovering Herefordshire Churches*

Mason E.J., *The Wye Valley, From River Mouth to Hereford*

Tonkin J.W., *Herefordshire*

Watkins A., *The Old Standing Crosses of Herefordshire.*

INDEX